Interpretation Made Simple

A Guide That Anyone Can Follow

Biblical Interpretation Made Simple

A Guide That Anyone Can Follow

Jerry F. Hutchins, M.A., M.Div.

NILES, ILLINOIS

Printed in the United States of America

Printed by:
Mall Publishing Company
5731 West Howard Street
Niles, Illinois 60714
877.203.2453

Cover Design by Andrew Ostrowski

Book Design by Marlon B. Villadiego

Unless otherwise noted, all scripture quotations are from the King James Version (KJV) of the Holy Bible.

Quotations from The New American Standard Bible (NASB) are used with permission from the Lockman Foundation.
http://www.lockman.org

ISBN 0-9748686-6-3

For licensing / copyright information, for additional copies or for use in specialized settings contact:

Jerry F. Hutchins Ministries, Inc.
P.O. Box 81879
Conyers, Georgia 30013
www.jerryhutchins.org

COMMENDATIONS

"Without the proper study methods, reading and understanding the Bible can be a challenge. With Biblical Interpretation Made Simple, Jerry F. Hutchins provides readers with a proven method of getting the most out of the Scriptures, using the guidance of the Holy Spirit and numerous easy-to-follow techniques."

Bishop Eddie L. Long
Senior Pastor, New Birth Missionary Baptist Church
Lithonia, Georgia

"This book is a great tool for anyone seeking to teach the Bible or enhance their personal study of God's Word. Laypersons and ministers alike will definitely gain greater understanding of how to correctly understand what the Scriptures say, as well as what they mean."

Dr. Samuel R. Chand
Chancellor, Beulah Heights Bible College
Atlanta, Georgia

TABLE OF CONTENTS

ACKNOWLEDGEMENTS

I would like to thank the many people who have encouraged me to write this book.

To my wife, Sheila, thank you for your patience and support of me in all of my ministry functions. I appreciate your love and the sacrifice you make.

To my daughter, Kisha, and my son-in-law, Patrick, thank you for keeping me reminded that the task had to be done and offering your services without hesitation.

To my mother, Bell and my siblings for being the family that you are.

Thank you Timothy Baptist Church for your prayers and being the followers that you are. Thank you for pushing me forward to destiny.

INTRODUCTION

Teachers in the Christian Church have been spoiled by the overwhelming use of commentaries. For many, the commentary has become their substitute for the Bible itself. It is not at all uncommon for a Sunday school teacher or a Bible study instructor to study the entire lesson from the commentary and never pick up the Bible.

Bible commentaries try to clarify the meaning of biblical texts by providing relevant background information and by discussing issues involved in interpreting those texts. In a sense, a commentary is a digest of information that might be found more completely in other works; historical, geographical, and archaeological data; linguistic, text critical, and literary comments; summaries of debate and discussion over the interpretation of a text; contemporary application of a text; and more. Because so much is gathered in one place, commentaries are handy. But because they are digests rather than full accounts of relevant information, they are not suitable substitutes for complete exegetical research.

The average teacher in the Christian Church has not been equipped with the tools and skills to do a completed exegetical research of a text. The idea of interpreting for one's self is intimidating. Reading the Bible and developing an interpretation of the text is more than most teachers want to do. It is much easier to go to the commentary and teach what they say, whether it is right or wrong.

Commentaries are simply comments made by other people. Commentaries give the reader the viewpoint of the writer. The writer has exercised the principles of hermeneutics and reached his personal interpretation of the text. His interpretation is not independent of his religious background and other exposures that influence his thinking.

The teacher should practice the same approach to the text and determine what it means before consulting a commentary. The fire to teach what we have interpreted for ourselves is much more intense than the fire we have to teach what the commentary says.

A commentary is a convenient resource for Bible study because it presents the end result of scholarly research in a concise form and in biblical order. But if you consult only the end result for its convenient answers, you do not learn how to study for yourself. In addition, the commentary may not have the answers you need.

This book provides the teacher with basic skills for

interpreting scripture. You will see your teaching go to a greater dimension as you practice these skills and bring meaning out of the text.

1

START WITH A GOOD TRANSLATION

It is vitally important that the Biblical interpreter start with a good translation of the Bible. All translations have an intended purpose, but all are not good to begin the process of interpreting scripture. Having basic knowledge of the history of the Bible helps the interpreter apply the principles of hermeneutics.

An English version of the Bible did not exist until a little more than 600 years ago. Before then, a version translated into Latin by Jerome in the fourth century, called the Latin Vulgate, was the most widely used Bible translation in the Middle-Ages. Portions of scripture in English began to emerge in the early seventh century. However, the first complete English translation, by the influence of John Wycliff, was not produced until 1382. Despite fierce opposition of the Roman church, and absence of the printing press, copies of this work were widely circulated.

Later in the 16th century, seven more popular English versions were produced, beginning with William Tyndale's work in 1525. This English version of the New Testament was the first to be translated directly from the Greek instead of Latin texts. After Tyndale, several other famous Bibles were produced in the 16th century: The Cloverdale Bible in 1535, Matthew's Bible in 1537, The Great Bible in 1539, The Geneva Bible in 1560, and the Bishops Bible in 1568.

Finally in 1604, in an effort to resolve severe factions between Englishmen over Bible versions, King James I authorized the translation of another version that came to bear his name. Forty-seven scholars spent six years on the translation, with all work meticulously reviewed and refined by their combined collaboration. The King James Version was finally published in 1611, and together with its four revisions (in 1629, 1638, 1762, and 1769), it remains as the most widely circulated Bible in existence.

A few other translations were produced over the centuries, but the real revolution of new Bible versions began to erupt in the 20th century, largely due to the widening language barrier. Some of the more influential, recent translations have been: The Revised Standard Version in 1952, The Amplified Bible in 1965, The New English Bible in 1970, The New American Standard Bible in 1971, The Living Bible in 1971, Today's English Version in 1976, The New International Version in 1978, and the New King James Version in 1982.

Apart from these versions, there are numerous study Bible editions, such as The Scofield Reference Bible, The Open Bible, The Thompson Chain Reference Bible, or The Spirit Life Bible, etc., but these are not different translations. These volumes merely feature special study helps, commentaries or references added as a supplement to a particular translation.

In the late 1970's, Thomas Nelson Publishers commissioned a company of scholars to produce a revision of the traditional King James Version. Relying on the familiar Textus Receptus, 130 translators made the needed revisions to modern English and corrections to minor translation errors, while making every effort to retain the traditional phraseology of the old version. This New King James Version, as it was called, was completed in 1982.

SUMMARY OF BIBLE VERSIONS

The following is a summary of the most popular versions, along with a brief evaluation:

THE KING JAMES VERSION (KJV)

The King James Version (KJV) - Translated in 1611 by 47 scholars using the Byzantine family of manuscripts, Textus Receptus. The Byzantine Family of manuscripts tend to be secondary sources (copies of other manuscripts), sometimes called the Koine family. Favored by the Greek Orthodox Church, hence the term Byzantine, but since it combines elements from earlier types of texts, is considered inferior in part to other families. This remains as a good version of the Bible. It has been the most reliable translation for over three centuries, but its Elizabethan style Old English is difficult for modern readers, especially youth, to understand. This is still a good translation for those who can deal with the language.

THE NEW AMERICAN STANDARD BIBLE (NASB)

The New American Standard Bible (NASB) -

Translated in 1971 by 58 scholars of the Lockman Foundation, from Kittle's Biblia Hebraica and Nestle's Greek New Testament 23rd ed., which include the Alexandrian Family codices. The Alexandrian Family codices are generally considered the most carefully prepared manuscript or text types. Though academic in tone, The New American Standard Bible is said to be the most exact English translation available.

THE LIVING BIBLE (TLB)

The Living Bible (TLB) - A paraphrased rendition of the King James Version by Kenneth Taylor in 1971. This is not a genuine translation, but is a type of phrase-by-phrase commentary that was originally intended to help the author's own children understand the scriptures. It is useful for inspiration and commentary, but for serious Bible study it should only be used in conjunction with a legitimate translation.

The New International Version (NIV) - Over 100 translators completed this work in 1978, which was composed from Kittle's, Nestle's and United Bible Society's texts, which include the Alexandrian Family codices. This is considered an "open" style translation. It is a good, easy to read version.

THE NEW KING JAMES VERSION (NKJV)

The New King James Version (NKJV) - 130 translators, commissioned by Thomas Nelson Publishers, produced this version from the Byzantine Family (Textus Receptus) in 1982. This is a revision of the King James Version, updated to modern English with minor translation corrections and retention of traditional phraseology. This is a very good version.

UNDERSTANDING BIBLE TRANSLATIONS

The Bible was originally written in three different languages. Most of the Old Testament was originally written in Hebrew. Parts of Ezra and Daniel were written in Aramaic. The entire New Testament was originally written in Greek. Since most of us are not familiar with these languages it is important that we have a translation of the Bible that is as accurate as possible.

Each version of the Bible has been translated using one of three theories of translation.

LITERAL TRANSLATIONS

Literal translations attempt to translate by keeping

as close as possible to the exact words and phrasing in the original language, yet still make sense in the receptor language. The King James Version and the New American Standard are considered literal translations.

This is how part of Genesis reads as it is literally translated.

Genesis 1:1

In the beginning | created | God | the heavens | and | the earth

Genesis 1:2

and the earth | was | without form | and empty, | and darkness | on the surface of | the deep | and the Spirit of | God | moving gently | on | the surface of | the waters.

Genesis 1:3

Then said | God, | Let be | light | and was | light.

Genesis 1:4

And saw | God | the light | that | (it was) | good | and separated | God | between | the light | and | the darkness.

Genesis 1:5

And called | God | the light | day, | and the darkness | He called | night | and was | evening, | and (it) was | morning, | day | one.

The American Standard Bible was printed as a literal translation.

1:1 In the beginning God created the heavens and the earth. 1:2 And the earth was waste and void; and darkness was upon the face of the deep: and the Spirit of God moved upon the face of the waters 1:3 And God said, Let there be light: and there was light. 1:4 And God saw the light, that it was good: and God divided the light from the darkness. 1:5 And God called the light Day, and the darkness he called Night. And there was evening and there was morning, one day.

Since its completion in 1971, the New American Standard Bible has been widely acclaimed as "the most literally accurate translation" from the original languages. Millions of people, students, scholars, pastors, missionaries, and laypersons alike, have trusted the New American Standard Bible, learning from it and applying it to the challenges of their daily lives. With the New American Standard Bible, anyone can discover what the original text really says, word for word, because it is considered the most literal translation of the Bible in the English language, consistently following the oldest and best manuscripts.

The New American Standard Bible update continues this commitment to accuracy, while increasing clarity and readability. Vocabulary, grammar, and sentence structure have been carefully updated for greater understanding and smoother reading. The updated New American Standard Bible remains the most literally accurate Bible in the English language.

FREE TRANSLATION

Free Translation, also called paraphrase, attempts to translate the ideas from one language to another, with less concern about using the exact words of the original.

A very popular paraphrase translation is the Amplified Bible.

The Amplified Bible is a translation that, by using synonyms and definitions, both explains and expands the meaning of words in the text by placing amplification in parentheses and brackets after key words or phrases. This unique system of translation allows the reader to more completely grasp the meaning of the words, as they were understood in the original languages. Through multiple expressions, fuller and more revealing appreciation is given to the divine message as the original text legitimately permits.

The Amplified Bible is free of personal interpretation and is independent of denominational prejudice. It is a translation from the accepted Hebrew, Aramaic, and Greek manuscripts into literary English. It is based on the American Standard Version of 1901, Rudolph Kittel's Biblia Hebraica, the Greek text of Westcott and Hort, and the 23rd edition of the Nestle Greek New Testament as well as the best Hebrew and Greek lexicons available at the time. Cognate languages, the Dead Sea Scrolls, and other Greek works were also consulted. The Septuagint and other versions were compared for interpretation of textual differences. In completing the Amplified Bible, translators made a determined effort to keep, as far as possible, the familiar wording of the earlier versions, and especially the feeling of the ancient Book. Through amplification, the reader gains a better understanding of what the Hebrew and Greek listener instinctively understood (as a matter of course).

The Living Bible Paraphrased is also a free translation. Kenneth Taylor, not being a scholar, was unable to translate from Hebrew and Greek. He used English versions as the basis of this paraphrase. In an interview he stated that in this he used chiefly the American Standard Version (1901) as his basic text. The preface states that scholars reviewed the work, but the names of these scholars are not given.

Taylor created this paraphrase as help for those who wanted to read the Bible to children without having to stop and explain many things. He founded Tyndale House Publishers for the purpose of publishing the work, beginning with the Epistles as Living Letters in 1962. In the following year the evangelist Billy Graham offered Taylor's paraphrase as a television premium on broadcasts of his popular "Crusades," and this brought the book into prominence. Taylor proceeded to paraphrase the entire New Testament (published in 1967), and then the Old Testament (1971). Many thousands of copies were distributed at Graham's crusades during the 1970's and 1980's, and it became a widely used Bible, marketed as a version for adults.

Despite its great popularity (Tyndale House reports that by 1997 its sales of the Living Bible had exceeded 40 million copies), very few scholars have given any encouragement to its use, and many have strictly warned against it.

Free translations are good for casual reading but should not be used for the interpretive process.

DYNAMIC EQUIVALENT TRANSLATIONS

Dynamic equivalent translations attempt to translate words, idioms, and grammatical constructions of the original language into precise equivalents in the receptor language. These translations keep the historical distance on all historical and most factual matters, but updates matters of language, grammar, and style.

The New International Version is considered a dynamic equivalent translation.

The New International Version is a translation of the Holy Bible made by over a hundred scholars working directly from the best available Hebrew, Aramaic and Greek texts. It had its beginning in 1965 when, after several years of exploratory study by committees from the Christian Reformed Church and the National Associations of Evangelicals, a group of scholars met at Palos Heights, Illinois, and concurred in the need for a new translation of the Bible in contemporary English. This group, though not made up of official church representatives, was transdenominational. Its conclusion was endorsed by a large number of leaders from many denominations who met in Chicago in 1966.

Responsibility for the new version was delegated by the Palos Heights group to a self-governing body of fifteen, the Committee on Bible Translation, composed for the most part of biblical scholars from colleges, universities and seminaries. In 1967 the New York Bible Society (now the International Bible Society) generously undertook the financial sponsorship for the project - sponsorship that made it possible to enlist the help of many distinguished scholars. The fact that participants from the United States, Great Britain, Canada, Australia and New Zealand worked together gave the project its international scope. That they were from many denominations - including Anglican, Assemblies of God, Baptist, Brethren, Christian Reformed, Church of Christ, Evangelical Free, Lutheran, Mennonite, Methodist, Nazarene, Presbyterian, Wesleyan and other churches - helped to safeguard the translation from sectarian bias.

How it was made helps to give the New International Version its distinctiveness. The translation of each book was assigned to a team of scholars. Next, one of the Intermediate Editorial Committees revised the initial translation, with constant reference to the Hebrew, Aramaic or Greek. Their work then went on to one of the General Editorial committees, which checked it in detail and made another thorough version. The Committee on Bible Translation, which made further changes and then released the final version for publication, in turn carefully, reviewed this revision. In this way the entire Bible underwent three revisions, during each of which the translation was examined for its faithfulness to the original languages and for its English style.

All of this involved many thousands of hours of research and discussion regarding the meaning of the texts and the precise way of putting them into English. It may well be that no other translation has been made by a more thorough process of review and revision from committee to committee than this one.

From the beginning of the project, the Committee on Bible Translation held to certain goals for the New International Version: that it would be an accurate translation and one that would have clarity and literary quality and so prove suitable for public and private reading, teaching, preaching, memorizing and liturgical use. The Committee also sought to preserve some measure of continuity with the long tradition of translating the Scriptures into English.

In working toward these goals, the translators were united in their commitment to the authority and infallibility of the Bible as God's Word in written form. They believe that it contains the divine answer to the deepest needs of humanity, that it sheds unique light on our path in a dark world, and that it sets forth the way to our eternal well being.

The first concern of the translators has been the accuracy of the translation and its fidelity to the thought of the biblical writers. They have weighed the significance of the lexical and grammatical details of the Hebrew, Aramaic and Greek texts. At the same time, they have striven for more than a word-for-word translation. Because thought patterns and syntax differ from language to language, faithful communication of the meaning of the writers of the Bible demands frequent modifications in sentence structures and constant regard for the contextual meaning of words.

A sensitive feeling for the style does not always accompany scholarship. Accordingly, the Committee on Bible Translation submitted the developing version to a number of stylistic consultants. Two of them read every book of both Old and New Testaments twice - once before and once after the last major revision - and made invaluable suggestions. Samples of the translations were tested for clarity and ease of reading by various kinds of people - young and old, highly educated and less well educated, ministers and laymen.

The best approach to Biblical interpretation is to begin with a dynamic equivalent translation and a literal translation. Use both of them. The literal translation may be more challenging to read; however, it will offer greater accuracy of the original wordings. A dynamic equivalent will use equivalent words that are more easily understood in the receptor language and when used along side a literal translation, hermeneutics becomes an exciting endeavor.

If you must choose between a King James Version, New American Standard Version, or New King James Version for your literal translation, use the New American Standard Version and New King James Version first. The New King James Version has updated and corrected the original King James. New does not necessarily mean better, but when it comes to Bible versions, allow "new" to be an indication that it offers what the old one did not.

When you sit at your desk with a good New International Version of the Bible, a good New King James Version and a good New American Standard Version, you are ready to go to the next level in interpreting scripture.

2

THE OBSERVATION PROCESS

READ THE TEXT FOR WHAT IT SAYS

NOW THAT YOU have Bibles at your disposal, read the text being examined. After you have read the text, read the text again. After you have read it again, read it some more. After you have read it some more, read it over. Read it at least ten times before you even begin to try understanding the meaning. You are reading the text to see what it says. This is called the observation phase of Biblical interpretation. You are reading to see what the Bible says because failure to understand what it says, will keep you from understanding what it means.

As you are reading through the text ten times or more, jot down the things that jump out at you. There will be certain things in every passage that stand out more obviously than others.

Write down the obvious. In this phase of the process you will be writing down key words (theological terms like justification, sanctification, regeneration, salvation, faith, etc.).

Observe people, places and the events of the passage. You will also take note of the verbs. By noting the verbs you will be able to feel the action that is going on in the passage.

Don't overlook any characters in the passage. Write down their names and the action that they give to the passage.

Spending this kind of time reading the passage will cause you to become a part of the event. This process is intended to draw you into the text and once in it you will clearly see what's going on.

OBSERVE THE FACTS

During the observation phase of Biblical interpretation, interrogate the text. Bombard the text with questions. The 5 W's and an H that you have applied in other interrogations are just as effective in Biblical interpretation.

Who is the writer? Who is speaking? Who are the

major and minor characters? Who is the speaker talking to? Who is the speaker talking about?

What are the main events? What are the major ideas? What is the context of the text? What are the major teachings? What is the theme of the passage? What is God (or the trinity) doing in this passage? What type of genre is this? What does this word mean?

When was it written? When did the event take place? If future prophesies, when will the event take place?

Where did the event occur? Where are the people? Where is the writer? Where is the speaker? If prophecy, where will the event occur?

Why was the text written? Why is so little or so much space devoted to this event? Why is it mentioned here?

How did the event happen? How will the event happen? How did the people in the text receive this teaching?

OBSERVE REPETITIONS

Note identical words or phrases, or similar ideas and themes that appear in the passage. For instance, the Lord's repeated use of the word "blessed" in the Beatitudes (Matthew 5:3-11).

OBSERVE CONTRASTS

These are often easily identified by the use of "but" or "rather." For instance, Jesus' teaching on righteousness in the Sermon on the Mount, as in: You have heard that it was said, 'Do not commit adultery.' But I tell you that anyone who looks at a woman lustfully has already committed adultery with her in his heart (Matthew 5:27-28).

OBSERVE CAUSE AND EFFECT

This is where one thing causes, affects, or changes another. In Matthew 5:19 there are two: Anyone who breaks one of the least of these commandments and teaches others to do the same will be called least in the kingdom of heaven, but whoever practices and teaches these commands will be called great in the kingdom of heaven.

OBSERVE THE NEED FOR DEFINITIONS

Mark words or phrases the meaning of which should be carefully explored. For example, the less-than-commonly-used description of Christ used by the apostle John: And he is the propitiation for our sins: and not for ours only, but also for the sins of the whole world (1 John 2:2).

OBSERVE EXPLANATIONS

This is where something is defined, examined, explained, or analyzed within the text itself. Like the Apostle Paul's discussion of love in 1 Corinthians 13, or in Mark 4 where Jesus first tells a parable and then explains what he means: Listen! A farmer went out to sow his seed... The farmer sows the word (vs. 3 & 14).

OBSERVE GENERAL/PARTICULAR

Identify where there is movement in the text from a broad idea or concept to a specific one (or vice versa). For example, when the apostle James first states a general principle and then discusses a particular illustration: My brothers, as believers in our glorious Lord Jesus Christ, don't show favoritism. Suppose a man comes into your meeting wearing a gold ring and fine clothes, and a poor man in shabby clothes also comes in... (2:1-2).

OBSERVE INTERROGATION

This involves any use of questions and/or answers within the text. As in when the Lord God asked Job a whole series of questions: Then the LORD answered Job out of the storm. He said: "Who is this that darkens my counsel with words without knowledge? Brace yourself like a man; I will question you, and you shall answer me. Where were you when I laid the earth's foundation? Tell me, if you understand" (Job 38:1-4).

OBSERVE DESCRIPTIONS

Note the adjectives, adverbs, or any other modifiers used. There are a lot of these in the Song of Songs:

How beautiful you are, my darling! Oh, how beautiful!

Your eyes behind your veil are doves.

Your hair is like a flock of goats descending from Mount Gilead.

Your teeth are like a flock of sheep just shorn, coming up from the washing.

Each has its twin; not one of them is alone.

Your lips are like a scarlet ribbon; your mouth is lovely.

Your temples behind your veil are like the halves

of a pomegranate (4:1-3).

OBSERVE CLIMAX

This involves any arrangement of material in a progression. Like Peter's discussion of Christian maturity: For this very reason, make every effort to add to your faith goodness; and to goodness, knowledge; and to knowledge, self-control; and to self-control, perseverance; and to perseverance, godliness; and to godliness, brotherly kindness; and to brotherly kindness, love (2 Peter 1:5-7).

OBSERVE VERBS

The verbs used throughout the text often provide insight into the action and/or characteristics of the subject being discussed. Tracing the verbs in a passage is crucial to unpacking the text's meaning.

OBSERVE PRONOUNS

The use of pronouns is often crucial to identifying the narrator and/or understanding the perspective inherent in the text. For instance, just who is declaring the rather chilling conclusion in Psalm 137:8-9? Is it

God? Or the grieving parent?

O Daughter of Babylon,
doomed to destruction,
happy is he who repays you for what you have done to us-
he who seizes your infants and dashes them against the rocks.

OBSERVE INTERCHANGES

This refers to any alternating or exchanging of elements in the text, so that persons, events, or ideas end up being compared or contrasted, implicitly or explicitly. The first few chapters of 1 Samuel tell the stories of Hannah and her son Samuel, and Eli and his sons. The contrast, though implicit, is unmistakable.

OBSERVE QUOTATIONS

Identify where the text contains quotations of other passages of Scripture, or extra-biblical books, or where this text is quoted elsewhere in the Bible. For instance, Paul quoted (and agreed with) the Stoic poet Aratus in Acts 17: "For in him we live and move and have our being." As some of your own poets have said, "We are his offspring." (vs. 28).

As you make these observations in the text, you will begin unpacking and identifying what is there so you can begin interpreting its meaning (which is, of course, the next step in the process of Bible study). In fact, as you observe you'll probably note that interpretation comes naturally. You'll wrestle with what the observations mean, look up words with which you are unfamiliar, and begin to note the flow of thought of the author. Sometimes, just spending time in careful observation will open the text to you in fresh and wonderful ways.

During the observation phase of Biblical interpretation, you are bombarding the text with questions but you are not answering the questions. If you stop and try to answer the questions before you have thoroughly read the text, you are vulnerable to misinterpretation. The natural instinct is to go ahead and answer the questions based on ideas that we have developed previously. Our previous ideas may be wrong and they will block us from receiving the truth that God intends to expose as we interpret what He is saying. Even our traditional and denominational teachings are subject to flaw. We do not grow and develop by trying to hold on to traditions and denominational teachings. We grow by feeding ourselves with the truth of God's word.

3

METHODS OF INTERPRETATION

THERE ARE MANY different methods of interpreting Scripture. Unfortunately, some of those methods can cause the interpreter to put into the text rather than extract from the text. These methods of interpretation are very popular. Preachers and teachers use these methods often and listeners applaud them as being deep theologians. However, these approaches are dangerous and can seriously mislead people. It would ease the seriousness of the problem if the interpreter would indicate the method that he has used to reach his conclusion. If that were done, the people would know that the presentation is not necessarily what the Bible says, but it is a method of interpretation that the presenter used to make his point.

One such method of interpretation is the allegorical method. The allegorical method originated through the union of Greek philosophy and religion. With the rise of philosophy, the Greeks began to realize that they could not interpret their religious writings literally and still hold to their philosophy. If both were taken literally they would be contradictory. Because of their new found loyalty to philosophy they had to conclude, in order to reconcile the two, that their religious writings meant something other than what they literally said.

The allegorical method is motivated by the thought that the text has a hidden meaning. Preachers and teachers often feel a need to dig beyond the literal meaning of a text to expose, what they consider, a spiritual truth. When the text is read, the allegorical approach inserts spiritual meanings in place of literal things and often the insertion says what the text never intended.

The allegorical method of biblical interpretation is also sometimes called "spiritualizing the text." Rev. William E. Currie tells of how one of his seminary professors used this method in a class. He says "in a class on Revelation in a seminary holding to the allegorical method, a professor I know of taught that there will be no literal millennial period with a literal reign of Messiah on earth." He stated that the thousand years referred to in Revelation 20:2 only speaks of this long period of time for the present age before Messiah returns to begin eternity. When a student asked about the text that says Satan will be bound for that "long period of time," the professor replied, "Satan is bound today, but with a long chain." The allegorical method is free to look beyond the literal words of the text to see another meaning.

The allegorical method should not be confused with typology. The former uses inserts or replacements performed without any Biblical proof of its relevance. It searches for secondary and hidden meanings underlying the primary and obvious meaning of a historical narrative. The latter is a preordained representative relationship, which certain persons, events, and institutions bear to corresponding persons, events, and institutions occurring at a later time in salvation history. One key word that makes the distinction is "preordained."

In Romans 5:19, Adam is presented as a legitimate type of Christ. "For as by one man's disobedience many were made sinners, so by the obedience of one shall many be made righteous."

In John 3:14, Moses is presented as a type of Christ

and the lifting of the serpent as a type of the crucifixion. "And as Moses lifted up the serpent in the wilderness, even so must the Son of man be lifted up."

Matthew 24:37 presents the flood as a type of the second coming of Christ. "But as the days of Noe [were], so shall also the coming of the Son of man be."

The Bible is loaded with types. Proper exegesis brings the types out of Scripture. Poorly performed eisegesis puts meanings into the Scripture. Good interpreters of Scripture always practice exegesis and never eisegesis.

The oldest and most accurate method of interpreting Scripture is the literal method. Kevin Connor states that "the literal method assumes that the words of Scripture in their plain evident meaning are reliable; that God intended His revelation to be understood by all who believe; that the words of Scripture communicate what God wants man to know; and that God based the communication of truth on the regular laws governing written communication, thereby intending for it to be interpreted by those same laws".

We must avoid interpreting any text different from the way the author intended it to be received. If the author intended it to be figurative, then we should interpret it accordingly. If the author is presenting a symbol in the text, then the symbol must be interpreted as a symbol. We should never sway from the intended meaning. Even when we interpret figures and symbols as the author intended, we are still in essence applying the literal method of interpretation. A figurative word is to be literally interpreted to be figurative. A symbol is to be literally interpreted as a symbol. This may sound like an oxymoron but it presents the truth of accurate biblical interpretation.

Probably, the thing that causes Bible readers to eisegete versus exegete scripture is the desire to make the text say something to the reader. Since the text does not seem to say anything to us as it reads, there is a tendency to insert a meaning. We should first observe the text for what it says. Secondly, interpret the text for what it means. That completes the hermeneutical process. A final step that is exercised is application. The application is not a part of hermeneutics but readers rush to make application without first applying proper hermeneutics.

Application is the articulate process by which truth is brought to bear directly and personally upon individuals in order to persuade them to respond properly to it. Application is more of a preaching (homiletics) responsibility than it is a teaching (hermeneutics) responsibility. Preaching expands hermeneutics to the point of persuading the listener to respond to what he has been taught. Teaching is responsible for giving information but does not necessarily persuade the student to respond. Every preacher must teach but every teacher does not necessarily preach.

Application is the "how to" of the text. Interpretation answers the question, "What does the text mean to the people in the text?" Application answers the question, "What does the text mean to the reader and how is it lived out?" Observation answers the question, "What does the text say?" Observation and interpretation looks for meaning to the people in the text. Application takes what the text means to them and then applies the principle to the life of the reader. Do not approach the text looking for the application until observation and interpretation has been properly carried out.

4

THE INTERPRETATION PROCESS

AFTER YOU HAVE read the text to see what it says, you are now ready to start interpreting the text. Interpretation moves us from reading what the text says to determining what the text means. What it says can sound one way but the meaning can be entirely different.

I CORINTHIANS 11:1-16

"Imitate me, just as I also imitate Christ. 2 Now I praise you, brethren, that you remember me in all things and keep the traditions just as I delivered them to you. 3 But I want you to know that the head of every man is Christ, the head of woman is man, and the head of Christ is God. 4 Every man praying or prophesying, having his head covered, dishonors his head. 5 But every woman who prays or prophesies with her head uncovered dishonors her head, for that is one and the same as if her head were shaved. 6 For if a woman is not covered, let her also be shorn. But if it is shameful for a woman to be shorn or shaved, let her be covered. 7 For a man indeed ought not to cover his head, since he is the image and glory of God; but woman is the glory of man. 8 For man is not from woman, but woman from man. 9 Nor was man created for the woman, but woman for the man. 10 For this reason the woman ought to have a symbol of authority on her head, because of the angels. 11 Nevertheless, neither is man independent of woman, nor woman independent of man, in the Lord. 12 For as woman came from man, even so man also comes through woman; but all things are from God. 13 Judge among yourselves. Is it proper for a woman to pray to God with her head uncovered? 14 Does not even nature itself teach you that if a man has long hair, it is a dishonor to him? 15 But if a woman has long hair, it is a glory to her; for her hair is given to her for a covering. 16 But if anyone seems to be contentious, we have no such custom, nor do the churches of God."

It is easy to read what this text says. It is not quite as easy to determine what it means.

I CORINTHIANS 14: 34-35

"Let your women keep silent in the churches, for they are not permitted to speak; but they are to be submissive, as the law also says. 35 And if they want to learn something, let them ask their own husbands at home; for it is shameful for women to speak in church."

Again we see a passage that is easily read for what it says. The problem the interpreter faces is determining what it means.

1 Timothy 2: 8-15 is another passage that is easy to read but what does it mean?

"I desire therefore that the men pray everywhere, lifting up holy hands, without wrath and doubting; 9 in like manner also, that the women adorn themselves in modest apparel, with propriety and moderation, not with braided hair or gold or pearls or costly clothing, 10 but, which is proper for women professing godliness, with good works. 11 Let a woman learn in silence with all submission. 12 And I do not permit a woman to teach or to have authority over a man, but to be in silence. 13 For Adam was formed first, then

Eve. 14 And Adam was not deceived, but the woman being deceived, fell into transgression. 15 Nevertheless she will be saved in childbearing if they continue in faith, love, and holiness, with self-control."

A Pastor was conducting a fairly heated meeting with the Deacons. During the meeting, one Deacon jumped to his feet waving the Bible at the Pastor and shouted, "What does the Bible say?" The Pastor shouted back, "I don't care what the Bible says!" The Deacon used that statement as his opportunity to rally the other Deacons to his side of the argument. Another Deacon stood and looked at the Pastor in awe and responded, "I can't believe you said that." The Pastor very calmly said to the entire group, "Brothers, it is not what the Bible says that matters, it's what the Bible means and while this Deacon has quoted what it says, he has no idea what it means and has consequently caused division."

DETERMINE THE HISTORICAL-CULTURAL BACKGROUND THE TEXT

Historical-cultural analysis considers the historical-cultural climate in which the author wrote.

One important principle of interpretation is that the meaning of the text is always the author's intended meaning. There are many applications of a text but only one true interpretation. The text always means what it has always meant. Determining what the text means first and foremost demands that we determine what it meant to the original recipients. Do not approach a Biblical text asking, "what does the text mean to me." Approach the text asking, "what does the text mean to those in the text."

Proverbs 22:28 says, "Remove not the ancient landmark which your fathers have set," (RSV). Our natural instinct is to approach the text from our culture and our understanding of landmarks. Consequently, we would interpret the passage to mean, "do not move the antique items that our forefathers put on the property to mark the land." In actuality, this proverb means "do not steal". The ancient landmark refers to the boundary marker that separated one man's land from his neighbor's. Without modern surveying techniques it was a relatively easy matter to increase one's acreage by moving such markers late in an evening. The prohibition is directed against a specific type of stealing.

Consider the comparisons of Matthew 5:32 "But I say unto you, That whosoever shall put away his wife, saving for the cause of fornication, causeth her to commit adultery: and whosoever shall marry her that is divorced committeth adultery; Mark 10:11 "And he saith unto them, Whosoever shall put away his wife, and marry another, committeth adultery against her; and Luke 16:18, "Whosoever putteth away his wife, and marrieth another, committeth adultery: and whosoever marrieth her that is put away from [her] husband committeth adultery." These verses are similar; however, Matthew writes to the Jews whereas Mark and Luke basically address Gentiles. The Jews would have been aware of laws regarding fornication that the Gentiles would not have been aware of. "Saving the cause of fornication" does not mean adultery as we have interpreted it to mean. Matthew and the Jews were well aware and lived by Deuteronomy 24:1, "When a man hath taken a wife, and married her, and it come to pass that she find no favour in his eyes, because he hath found some uncleanness in her: then let him write her a bill of divorcement, and give [it] in her hand, and send her out of his house."

Matthew 5:31-32 gives us what is called the "exception clause"--"saving for the cause of fornication." This is the verse that many people use to condone what is referred to as "the innocent party" divorce and remarriage. However, this is not the exception clause that many would like it to be. This exception is only written in the book of Matthew. The book of Matthew was written to the Jews and the Jewish custom was different from some other customs. When Mark writes about this same situation he does not mention this exception clause.

There is a difference between "adultery" and "fornication." "Adultery" is sexual relations between two married people (other than husband and wife). "Fornication" is sexual relations between two unmarried people. If a married man has relations with an unmarried woman then the man has committed "adultery," but the woman has committed "fornication."

Jesus says in Matthew: "And I say unto you, whosoever shall put away his wife, except it be for fornication..." The Jewish people had a special custom. The wedding actually had a two-part ceremony. When a boyfriend and girlfriend decided that they were for each other, the first stage of the wedding (or the engagement) was held. The friends and relatives were called together for an engagement ceremony that was witnessed just like a wedding ceremony. Everyone knew that from this time on, this boy and girl were meant for each other, but they were to still remain pure until they had gone through the second phase of the wedding. If, during this engagement period, either one found out that the other one had been unfaithful (committed fornication), a bill of divorcement was allowed to be written. To help prove this we find that Matthew (who was writing to the Jews) stated this about Joseph and Mary: "Now the birth of Jesus Christ was on this wise: When as His mother Mary was espoused [engaged] to Joseph, before they came together [before they were married and had relations], she was found with child of the Holy Ghost. Then Joseph her husband, being a just man, and not willing to make her a public example, was minded to put her away privily [write a "bill of divorcement"]. But while he thought on these things, behold, the angel of the Lord appeared unto him in a dream, saying Joseph, thou son of David, fear not to take unto thee Mary thy wife: for that which is conceived in her is of the Holy Ghost. And she shall bring forth a son, and thou shalt call His name JESUS: for He shall save His people from their sins. Now all this was done, that it might be fulfilled which was spoken of the Lord by the prophet, saying, Behold, a virgin shall be with child, and shall bring forth a son, and they shall call His name Emmanuel, which being interpreted is, God with us. Then Joseph being raised from sleep did as the angel of the Lord had bidden him, and took unto him his wife: And knew her not [did not have any relations with her] till she had brought forth her firstborn son:

and he called His name JESUS" (Matthew 1:18-25).

This type of situation is what is referred to in Matthew 5. If during the engagement period the man or the woman found out that his or her partner had been unfaithful to him, that man or woman could have a bill of divorcement written and would then be free to marry another person.

DETERMINE THE CONTEXT

A common saying among biblical interpreters is "a text without a context is a pretext". Whenever we interpret scripture without considering the context of the scripture, we conceal the true meaning of the text. A text presented independent of the context can be forced to say whatever the reader wants the text to say. Context signifies the connection of thought running through either the whole of Scripture, a Testament, a book of the Bible, or a particular passage.

I heard the story of a young man who had committed an act of fornication with his girlfriend. After falling into sin he felt that he should marry the young girl. He used 1 Corinthians 7:36 and believed that by marring the girl, he would have canceled the sin of fornication.

"But if any man think that he behaveth himself

uncomely toward his virgin, if she pass the flower of [her] age, and need so require, let him do what he will, he sinneth not: let them marry".

According to his interpretation, "any man" referred to himself and he had behaved himself uncomely toward his virgin (girlfriend). She had "passed the flower of her age" by reaching maturity and was now having sexual needs. Since he had committed the act, "he sinneth not, let them marry".

This is an extreme illustration but it helps us see the terrible misuse of scripture. "Any man" in the above text is not a boyfriend. "Any man" is the father of the girl. In that day it was not uncommon for a father to refuse to allow his daughter to marry. In the context, especially verses thirty-seven and thirty-eight, it is clear that Paul is referring to the father of the girl and not her boy friend. When the father reached a point of conviction and felt that it was wrong to keep his daughter from being married, Paul wanted the father to know that he had not sinned by releasing her. Paul encourages celibacy and singleness; however, he wanted to assure the father that releasing his daughter to be married is not a sin.

This is one of those verses that you must use your own skills of interpretation to interpret because even the translations of the Bible differ.

The New King James Translation presents it as:

"But if any man thinks he is behaving improperly toward his virgin, if she is past the flower of youth, and thus it must be, let him do what he wishes. He does not sin; let them marry. Nevertheless he who stands steadfast in his heart, having no necessity, but has power over his own will, and has so determined in his heart that he will keep his *virgin, does well. So then he who gives *her in marriage does well, but he who does not give her in marriage does better."

The New American Standard Bible translates the verse as follows:

But if any man thinks that he is acting unbecomingly toward his virgin {daughter,} if she is past her youth, and if it must be so, let him do what he wishes, he does not sin; let her marry. But he who stands firm in his heart, being under no constraint, but has authority over his own will, and has decided this in his own heart, to keep his own virgin {daughter,} he will do well. So then both he who gives his own virgin {daughter} in marriage does well, and he who does not give her in marriage will do better.

The Revised Standard Version is even different from these two."If any one thinks that he is not behaving properly toward his betrothed, if his passions are strong, and it has to be, let him do as he wishes: let them marry--it is no sin. But whoever is firmly established in his heart, being under no necessity but having his desire under control, and has determined this in his heart, to keep her as his betrothed, he will do well. So that he who marries his betrothed does well; and he who refrains from marriage will do better."

Bible Explorer's Guide by John Phillips teaches that there are three circles of context that demand attention. First there is the immediate context. The verses and chapters immediately surrounding a verse should be examined to determine its significance. That context invariably sheds light on the text. 1 Corinthians 7:36 would not be so difficult to interpret if the interpreter would utilize verses 37 and 38, the immediate context.

Kevin Connor calls this "The Passage Context." Each book of the Bible is divided subject-wise into passages, each consisting of a group of consecutive verses pertaining a particular subject. Any single sentence or verse within a passage must be interpreted in the light of the subject-context of that passage.

Second and equally important is the context of the book itself in which any given passage is found. Any text from a book of the Bible must be interpreted in the context of the entire book. Each book of the Bible has its own particular purpose, message, and style.

Third and finally, we must consider the context of the whole Bible. Because truth has been revealed progressively, no one passage of Scripture can be considered in isolation from other passages related to it. That is why a concordance is such a valuable Bible study tool. We should use it to see how cross-referencing Scripture sheds light on a subject.

In addition to these three, a fourth principle is also useful, "The Testament Context." Within the whole of Scripture the context of any verse is the testament in which it is found. Each of the two Testaments has its own distinctive character and emphasis. The general emphasis of the Old Testament is law; the emphasis of the New is grace. It is imperative that Scripture be interpreted in accordance with the testament that it appears.

The process of context interpretation is to interpret the verse by the passage; interpret the passage by the book; interpret the book by the testament; interpret the testament by the Bible.

SUMMARY OF RESOURCES FOR BIBLICAL INTERPRETATION

While you should make your own interpretation prior to consulting a commentary, Bible Dictionaries,

Bible Encyclopedias and Bible Handbooks should be utilized to gather historical and cultural information.

Bible dictionaries have articles on a wide range of biblical topics, including historical, cultural, biographical, and geographical issues.

The following are recommendations that will assist in this phase of interpreting scripture; however, the best commentary on the bible is the bible itself.

NEW BIBLE DICTIONARY

The New Bible Dictionary is a reference work ideally suited for people of all ages and backgrounds. This magnificent and comprehensive Bible dictionary has set the standard for evangelical Bible dictionaries for five decades.

ZONDERVAN'S COMPACT BIBLE DICTIONARY

This comprehensive reference tool for Bible students and teachers is arranged by topic and provides over 6,000 entries with more than 100,000 Scripture references. It also serves as a Bible dictionary, listing all proper names, places, objects, and events of the Bible along with their brief definition or description.

UNGER'S BIBLE DICTIONARY

Unger's Bible Dictionary has been one of the best-selling Bible dictionaries on the market since its introduction in 1957. The New Unger's Bible Dictionary is packed with the most current scholarship. More than 6700 entries are supplemented with detailed essays and dozens of charts to enhance your understanding of God's Word.

The New Unger's Bible Dictionary includes an outline of every book of the Bible and complete coverage of people and places of the Bible. It has been carefully revised with the most up-to-date archaeological, geological, and theological research. Readable, informative and clear, The New Unger's Bible Dictionary includes the most recent findings that will deepen your cultural and archaeological insight. Whatever Bible translation you enjoy, you'll want this study guide close by.

ZONDERVAN PICTORIAL BIBLE DICTIONARY

This is the best-selling one-volume Bible dictionary. More than 5,000 entries include discussions of historical, geographical, chronological, and biographical aspects of the Bible, as well as articles on theological subjects; more than 700 pictures are included as well.

INTERPRETERS DICTIONARY OF THE BIBLE

This book is the most comprehensive and up-to-date work of its kind. It draws fully upon man's accumulated knowledge of the Bible and other relevant data and documents. For educators and students it is a comprehensive reference.

THE INTERNATIONAL STANDARD BIBLE ENCYCLOPEDIA

Representing the scholarship of hundreds of evangelical contributors from many specialized fields of biblical research, this encyclopedia includes articles on the every person and place mentioned in the Bible; all the terms in the Bible that have theological or ethical meaning; and the transmission, study, and interpretation of the bible. Based on the Revised Standard Version, ISBE contains cross-reference entries for forms used in the King James Version and the New English Bible, making it readily accessible to a wider range of readers.

WYCLIFFE BIBLE ENCYCLOPEDIA

Every proper name and place mentioned in the Bible is discussed in this standard evangelical Bible encyclopedia, along with all the most important subjects in theology and biblical background. Numerous photographs, drawings, and diagrams have been included to provide the clearest possible presentation of the information.

BIBLE HANDBOOKS

Bible handbooks give introductions to each of the books of the Bible and then briefly survey the contents, chapter by chapter. Some also give background material, maps, charts, etc.

EERDMAN'S HANDBOOK TO THE BIBLE

This is a great tool to any serious or even casual student of the Bible. It is full of full-color photos of myriad items of interest, maps, charts, and historical excerpts of Biblical figures. The contents include photos of sites in modern day Israel, photos of archaeological sites such as digs at Ur, a reconstruction of what the Tabernacle might have looked like, a diagram of

Jerusalem, and much, much more. With over 600 pages, it is a very interesting book, whether you're reading it in detail, or just thumbing through it!

HALLEY'S BIBLE HANDBOOK

An excellent aid to anyone studying the Bible. Covers archaeological discoveries, abbreviated Bible commentary, church history.

THE NEW UNGER'S BIBLE HANDBOOK

The New Unger's Bible Handbook is not a random collection of miscellaneous facts. It is carefully organized to form a commentary on God's Word, with an introduction, outline, and discussion of each book and its relationship to the complete biblical revelation. It gives a comprehensive yet concise introduction to the Bible, including its historical and archaeological background. It provides a history of the formation and preservation of the Bible, an outline of the intertestamental period, pertinent statistics, a synopsis of church history, and a survey of other religions.

5

UNDERSTADING THE WORD IN THE TEXT

LITERARY CONTEXT IS the thought element of any given passage. It is impossible to understand the meaning of a passage without understanding the meaning of the words that constitute the passage. Literary context goes beyond simply knowing what a word means. It is imperative that we know what the word means in the context of its usage in the passage being studied.

The Bible was originally written in Hebrew, Greek, and some Aramaic, and then translated into English and other languages. In the process of interpretation, it often helps to go back to the original languages to gain greater insight and clarification.

The Old Testament was written primarily in Hebrew with some Aramaic. In 100 B.C. the Old Testament Hebrew and Aramaic was translated in Koine (common) Greek. This translation is referred to as the Septuagint (LXX).

The New Testament was first written in Koine (common) Greek, which was the legal language at that time. Although Koine Greek fell into disuse after about A.D. 300, scholars have produced a number of Greek study tools for the English reader of the Bible. These tools help us to understand what the original authors meant to convey.

Exciting things happen when we understand words as the original authors of the Bible understood those words. Studying word definitions do not only reveal the meaning as the author intended it, but it helps us to know the tense, voice and mood of the verbs. The Koine Greek of the New Testament has more verb tenses than English. Having a basic knowledge of Greek verb tenses will greatly enhance your ability to interpret scripture.

WORDS AND THEIR TENSES

In Koine Greek, if the writer is referring to an action that happened in past time, he could refer to it as either progressive by using the imperfect tense or as merely a simple occurrence, with no emphasis on the action's progress by using the aorist tense.

For action happening at the present time, only the present tense is available. The Bible is loaded with present tense verbs. The present tense represents a simple statement of factor reality viewed as occurring in actual time. In most cases this corresponds directly with the English present tense. Some phrases, which might be rendered as past tense in English, will often occur in the present tense in Greek. These are termed "historical presents," and such occurrences dramatize the event described as if the reader were there watching the event occur. Some English translations render such historical presents in the English past tense, while others permit the tense to remain in the present.

The future tense primarily refers to the future time. The future tense corresponds to the English future, and indicates the contemplated or certain occurrence of an event,which has not yet occurred. "For the Lord himself shall descend from heaven with a shout, with the voice of the archangel, and with the trump of God: and the dead in Christ shall rise first" (1 Thes 4:16) is an example of the future tense as "shall descend" and "shall rise" are both future tense verbs.

The perfect tense has to do with the completed

progress of an action and its corresponding finished results. That is, it shows a present state of affairs (from the writer's perspective), based upon an action in past time. Since the perfect tense is used less frequently than other tenses, it is exegetically more significant. When it does occur, there is usually a definite and deliberate reason it was chosen by the writer. The emphasis may be on the culmination of the action's progress or on the resulting state of affairs brought about by the action.

The perfect tense in Greek corresponds to the perfect tense in English, and describes an action which is viewed as having been completed in the past, once and for all, not needing to be repeated. Jesus' last cry from the cross, TETELESTAI ("It is finished!")is a good example of the perfect tense used in this sense, namely "It [the atonement] has been accomplished, completely, once and for all time."

The past perfect (pluperfect) tense is the same as in the perfect tense. The difference is that it refers to this 'completed' condition at some time in the past. John 19:22 is an example of a pluperfect tense word. Pilate said, "what I have written, I have written." It refers to a completed condition at some time in the past. The condition is completed and will not change. What Pilate had written in the past has not changed.

The use of the pluperfect is rare in the New Testament. When Jesus speaks and makes reference to Old Testament scripture by saying, "it is written", he most often used the pluperfect tense. "It is written" is a completed condition at some time in the past.

The explanation of the future perfect is much like the past perfect, only the completed state will exist at some time in the future rather than in the past. Its use is also very rare in the New Testament.

WORDS AND THEIR MEANINGS

When doing word study you will find that there are many Hebrew and Greek classes of words that translate to a single word in our English language. There are even four "classes" of the word "if", indicating whether it means true, false, maybe, or the writer just wishes it was true, but it's not.

Our English language does not always have an exact word to translate from the original language so the best available word is used. Consider how many words the Hebrews had for "praise".

Shabach - to address in a loud tone; to glory; triumph

Halal - to shine; to celebrate

Yadah - to hold out the hand, to throw; to worship

with extended hands

Todah - hands extended; sacrifice of praise, thanks; thanksgiving offering

Barak - to kneel, by implication to bless God; adoration

Zamar - to play; to make music; to touch strings; accompanied; to celebrate in song and music; by voice.

In our English Bibles, all of these are translated "praise" but we are exposed to a world of difference when we understand the word from the author's original intent.

The Koine Greek has vivid word pictures, language idioms, and delicate shades of meaning. Greek scholars state that it would take an average of six English words to precisely translate each Koine Greek word into English. The problem is, the Bible would then be six times as thick, and hardly anyone would read it.

Melissa Munro and Judith Couchman compiled a book, Discipleship Journal's Best Bible Study Methods. In it, they say, "the basic purpose for a word study is to discover the most appropriate meaning of a particular word and to understand how that meaning affects a passage as a whole. The encouraging part about doing word studies is this: they can be as elementary or as involved as the Bible student desires. Word studies can be as simple as following three easy steps with only a Bible in hand. Or they can be as complicated as a lexical and etymological study using original languages and Greek or Hebrew reference works. You decide the complexity needed based on the resources you have available, the time at hand, and the nature of the word itself."

The three steps that they suggest are: Step One: Determine meanings and uses of the word; Step Two: Determine the best definition of the word; and Step Three: State the passage's meaning of the word. When does the word "power" mean strength, authority, or ability? The context should be used to help understand the meaning in the passage.

"Ye shall receive power (might) after that the Holy Ghost has come upon you." (Acts 1:8)

"But as many as received him, to them gave he power (the right to act, authority) to become the sons of God, [even] to them that believe on his name" (John 1:12)

SUMMARY OF RESOURCES FOR WORD STUDIES

You do not have to know Hebrew, Greek or

Aramaic to conduct a good word study of a passage. The following is a list of resources to use as you study Biblical words. The descriptions of the resources are the descriptions from the back cover of the resource itself or some other advertisement. I am not providing this information as my personal opinion of the resource; however, I do recommend that the serious student of the Bible purchase any or all of them.

THE NEW STRONG'S EXHAUSTIVE CONCORDANCE OF THE BIBLE: CLASSIC EDITION

by James Strong

This research tool is the revised edition of the legendary classic that generations have come to depend on for biblical research. Nothing has been omitted from the original text published in 1890, but new supplementary material such as "The Laws of the Bible," "Teaching and Illustrations of Christ," and a "Harmony of the Gospels" has been added and existing material has been updated and improved. The "Topical Index" references thousands of verses relating to over 8,000 biblical subjects, names, places, things, concepts, events, and doctrines. In this main section of the concordance, scripture references are placed between a context line and the reference to either the Hebrew or Greek dictionary, making it easier to access all the features of the concordance at once. The most useful improvement is that variant spellings of proper names from modern versions have been cross-referenced. For instance, the person who uses the Revised Standard Version, the New International Version, or the New American Standard Version of the Bible can look up the modern word Abronah, which appears in these versions, and will be directed to Ebronah, the New King James spelling.

VINE'S COMPLETE EXPOSITORY DICTIONARY OF OLD AND NEW TESTAMENT WORDS: WITH TOPICAL INDEX

by W. E. Vine, Merrill F. Unger

Study the meaning of biblical words in the original languages-without spending years learning Greek or Hebrew. This classic reference tool has helped thousands dig deeper into the meaning of the biblical text. Explains over 6,000 key biblical words. Includes a brand new comprehensive topical index that enables you to study biblical topics thoroughly.

THE STRONGEST STRONG'S EXHAUSTIVE CONCORDANCE OF THE BIBLE

by James Strong, John R. Kohlenberger III, James A . Swanson

Like a redwood that towers above all other trees, The Strongest Strong's takes James Strong's classic concordance to unprecedented heights. Reflecting thousands of research hours, custom computer technology, and an exclusive database perfected over twenty years, The Strongest Strong's is packed with features that make it the last word in accuracy and usefulness. No other Strong's concordance can touch it. This is no mere study tool. Destined to become a foundational resource for Bible study the world over, The Strongest Strong's is a landmark in biblical reference works.

WHAT MAKES THIS STRONG'S THE STRONGEST?

Rebuilding Strong's time-honored concordance from the ground up, biblical research experts John Kohlenberger and James Swanson have achieved unprecedented accuracy and clarity. Longstanding errors have been corrected. Omissions filled in. Word studies simplified. Thoroughness and ease of use have been united and maximized.

Kohlenberger and Swanson have also added the Nave's Topical Bible Reference System--the world's most complete topical Bible, updated, expanded, and streamlined to meet the needs of today's Bible user. No other edition of Strong's or Nave's gives you all the information combined in The Strongest Strong's.

ZONDERVAN NIV EXHAUSTIVE CONCORDANCE

by Edward W. Goodrick, John R. Kohlenberger, Zondervan Publishing

Among concordances based on the New International Version, only one provides an exhaustive indexing of every appearance of every word in the NIV Bible: the Zondervan NIV Exhaustive Concordance. It supplies readers of the NIV with more detailed and accurate information than the renowned Strong's Exhaustive Concordance has provided for readers for the King James Version. The Zondervan NIV Exhaustive Concordance gives complete access to every word of the NIV text as well as to the Hebrew, Aramaic, and Greek from which the NIV was translated. Feature for feature, this Gold

Medallion award-winning volume is by far the finest, most thorough NIV-based concordance available.

KING JAMES NEW STRONG'S EXHAUSTIVE CONCORDANCE OF THE BIBLE

by James Strong, Strong/Thomas Nelson Publisher

This edition of the King James New Strong's Exhaustive Concordance of the Bible gives you all the classic features of the full-size concordance in a smaller, more convenient form. Includes words of Christ emphasized; Strong's numbering system; indexes every word of the King James Version including articles, conjunctions, and prepositions; dictionaries of Hebrew and Greek words; easy-to-read print.

ZONDERVAN NASB EXHAUSTIVE CONCORDANCE

by Zondervan Publishing

More than a Resource. A Cornerstone for Bible Study.

It's crucial to select a concordance that works with the Bible translation you use. If the New American Standard Bible, Updated Edition, is your translation of choice, then the Zondervan NASB Exhaustive

Concordance is indispensable. With over 400,000 entries listing every word in the updated NASB, it gives you a powerful and essential reference tool for scaling the heights and plumbing the depths of God's Word. It is to the NASB what the Zondervan NIV Exhaustive Concordance is to the New International Version.

THAYER'S GREEK-ENGLISH LEXICON OF THE NEW TESTAMENT: CODED WITH STRONG'S CONCORDANCE NUMBERS

by Joseph Thayer

For over a century, Thayer's has been lauded as one of the best New Testament lexicons available. Both accessible and thorough, it is a work suited for the student of New Testament Greek. Thayer's provides dictionary definitions for each word and relates each word to its New Testament usage and categorizes its nuances of meaning. Its exhaustive coverage of New Testament Greek words, as well as its extensive quotation of extra-biblical word usage and the wealth of background sources consulted and quoted, render Thayer's an invaluable resource.

GESENIUS' HEBREW AND CHALDEE LEXICON TO THE OLD TESTAMENT

by Samuel Prideaux Tregelles, Friedrich Heinri Gesenius, Wilhelm Gesenius, H. W. Gesenius.

This is a dictionary of Old Testament words, which is numerically coded to Strong's Concordance. This lexicon is helpful in finding the meanings and connotations of O.T. words when doing word studies to more fully understand the scriptures. An index listing many English words and where their Hebrew/Chaldee counterpart is located in this book is included.

There are many other concordances and dictionaries that may be used. The above list is simply a compilation of resources to give you an idea of what to look for.

GLOSSARY OF TERMS

There are some basis terms that every person who teaches the Bible should be familiar with. In this chapter we will define some words that will help the teacher teach the Bible more affectively.

ALLEGORY

Taking the literal meaning off story, discourse, or something written and giving it another spiritualized or non-literal meaning.

APOCRYPHA

The biblical books included in the Vulgate and accepted in the Roman Catholic and Orthodox canon but considered no canonical by Protestants because they are not part of the Hebrew Scriptures.

CANON

The books of the Bible officially accepted as Holy Scripture.

CONTEXT

The parts of a book, passage or verse, which shows the whole situation and relevant environment in which it is found.

EISEGESIS

A personal interpretation of a text (especially of

the Bible) using your own ideas.

ETYMOLOGY

That part of grammar, which relates to the changes in the form of the words in a language.

EXEGESIS

To draw out. A critical explanation of a text of portion of Scripture.

Biblical exegesis involves approaching the text and drawing out what the text means. The Bible is read for what it says but proper exegesis must be exercised in order to determine what it means. It is never enough to instruct people to do what the Bible says. We cannot do what it says until we know what it means.

EXPOSITORY

Setting forth facts, ideas, and an explanation from a detailed examination of a passage.

FORM CRITICISM

Form criticism is a technique of higher criticism that seeks the message of the New Testament by analyzing the literary forms in which the message is given.

GENRE

A kind of literary or artistic work.

It is important that the teacher identify the genre being studied. Proper interpretation of a text demands that you identify the kind of literature you are reading. There are several types of genre in the Bible.

Historical Books

The Pentateuch (Historical Books)

Genesis, Exodus, Leviticus, Numbers, Deuteronomy

Historical Prophets

Joshua, Judges, 1st and 2nd Samuel, 1st and 2nd Kings

Historical Writings

1st and 2nd Chronicles, Ezra, Nehemiah

Stories

Ruth, Esther

Wisdom Literature

Job, Psalms, Proverbs, Ecclesiastes, Song of Solomon

Major Prophets

Isaiah, Jeremiah, (Lamentations), Ezekiel, Daniel

Minor Prophets

Hosea, Joel, Amos, Obadiah, Jonah, Micah, Nahum, Habakkuk, Zephaniah, Haggai, Zechariah, Malachi

Gospels

Matthew, Mark, Luke, John

History

Acts

Pauline Letters

Romans, 1st and 2nd Corinthians, Galatians, Ephesians, Philippians, Colossians, 1st and 2nd Thessalonians, 1st and 2nd Timothy, Titus, Philemon

General Letters

Hebrews, James, 1st and 2nd peter, 1st, 2nd, and 3rd John, Jude

Apocalyptic Revelation

It is important to realize that there can be one type of genre within another genre. For example, within prophecy there can be apocalyptic genre as in the case of Daniel.

If the reader fails to properly identify the genre he will be mislead in his interpretation. History should be interpreted as history. It is dangerous when we approach a historical document and interpret it as doctrine. The historical accounts of Acts should not be interpreted as doctrinal instructions for the Church. Paul writes letters to the Church to teach doctrine. Acts records historical events relating to Paul's travel and we should avoid interpreting it otherwise.

HERMENEUTICS

The art and science of Biblical interpretation Hermeneutics is considered a science because it has rules and these rules can be classified into an orderly system. It is considered an art because communication is flexible, and therefore a mechanical and rigid application of rules will sometimes distort the true meaning of a communication. To be a good interpreter one must learn the rules of hermeneutics as well as the art of applying those rules.

We do not study hermeneutics so that we can boast our unique ability to get out of scripture what no one else has ever seen. If you interpret and then get what no one else has ever seen, conclude that your interpretation is wrong. God has not reserved the truth of His Word waiting for any one individual to be born and then reveal His truth to the world. Interpretation that aims at, or thrives on, uniqueness can usually be attributed to pride. Unique interpretations are usually wrong. The aim of good interpretation is to get the plain meaning of the text.

HIGHER CRITICISM

Higher criticism is the analysis and study of

scripture to determine its authorship, date of composition, literary structure, or meaning.

HYPERBOLE

A figure of speech in which exaggeration is used for emphasis or effect, as in "I could sleep for a year" or "This book weighs a ton."

IDIOM

A style or manner of expression peculiar to a given people

INTERPRETATION

The process of determining the meaning of something.

LEXICON

A vocabulary, or book containing an alphabetical arrangement of the words in a language or of a considerable number of them, with the definition of each; a dictionary; especially, a dictionary of the Greek, Hebrew, or Latin language.

LOWER CRITICISM

The study and analysis of manuscript evidence to determine the original wording of the original text of the scriptures. Lower criticism produces the text that is used by translators.

OBSERVATION

The act of seeing.

One of the first steps in Biblical interpretation is observation. Approach the text to see what it says. Once we see what it says then we progress into interpreting what it means. The Bible says, "thou shalt not kill", but what does that mean. The Bible says "women keep silent in the Church", but we cannot stop at what it says (observation) but we have to interpret it to determine what it means.

REDACTION CRITICISM

The systematic analysis of an author's techniques of integrating source material into a literary work. By studying narrative transitions, repeated themes, & organization of material, the redaction critic tries to clarify that author's personal views, the character of the original audience & the circumstances that prompted the composition.

SEPTUAGINT

A Greek version of the Hebrew Scriptures that dates from the 3rd century B.C., containing both a translation of the Hebrew and additional and variant material, regarded as the standard form of the Old Testament in the early Christian Church and still canonical in the Eastern Orthodox Church.

SYNTAX

Syntax is the study of the word in its grammatical setting showing its relation to other words.

TEXTUAL CRITICISM

The study of manuscripts or printings to determine the original or most authoritative form of a text, especially of a piece of literature.

TEXTUS RECEPTUS

Textus Receptus, or Received Text, is a printed Greek New Testament that provided the textual base for the vernacular translations of the Reformation period. First, the name itself is a Latin phrase that can be translated as the received or agreed upon text. It is a printed text, not a hand-copied manuscript. It was the Greek text available to translators during the time of the Reformation.

TYPOLOGY

A study of the preordained representative relationship which certain persons, events, and institutions bear to corresponding persons, events, and institutions occurring at a later time in salvation history.

VULGATE

The Latin edition or translation of the Bible made by Saint Jerome at the end of the fourth century A.D., now used in a revised form as the Roman Catholic authorized version.

BIBLIOGRAPHY

Burns, C. "Divorce and Remarriage." Landmark Independent Baptist Church. May 20, 2004. <http.//users.aol.com/libcfl/divorce.htm>

Connor, Kevin. And Ken Malmin. Interpreting The Scriptures. Portland, 1983.

Currie, William. "The Jews, The Gentiles, and The Church." November 1999. AMF International. May 20, 2004. <www.amfi.org/heartbeat/hb991115.htm>

Discipleship Journal's. Best Bible Study Methods. Colorado Springs: Navpress Books, 2002.

Fee, Gordon. And Douglas Stuart. How To Read The Bible For All Its Worth. Grand Rapids: Zondervan Publishing, 1993.

Haack, Denis. "Observation: Seeing What The Text Says." RansomFellowship.May 1, 2004. <www.ransomfellowship.org/B_observe.html>

"International Bible Society." About The NIV. June 1978. <www.gospelcom.net/ibs/niv/background.php>

Jones, Bob. "About The New Testament 'Koine' Greek." May 20, 2004. <www.Biblefood.com/koine.html>

"New American Standard Bible." Background and History <www.gospel.net/lockman/nasb/>

Philips, John. How To Understand and Interpret The Bible. Grand Rapids: Kregel Publications, 1987.

"Resources for learning New Testament Greek." Verb Tenses. May 18, 2004. <www.ntgreek.org/learn_nt_greek/grkindex.htm>

Robins, Dale, "Why So Many Bible Translations." 1995. Victorious Network. May 26, 2004. <www.victorious.org/translat.htm>

Samworth, Herbert, "What is Textus Receptus?" Sola Scriptura. May 26, 2004. <www.solagroup.org/articles/faqs/faq_0032.html>

Stein, Robert. A Basic Guide to Interpreting the Bible. Grand Rapids: Baker Books, 1999.

Taylor, Kenneth N. etal. The Living Bible, Paraphrased. Wheaton, Illinois: Tyndale House Publishers, 1971.

Virkler, Henry. Hermeneutics, Principles and Processes of Biblical Interpretation. Grand Rapids: Baker Books, 1981.

WORKBOOK AVAILABLE

Please Contact:

JERRY F. HUTCHINS MINISTRIES, INC.
P.O. Box 81879
Conyers, Georgia 30013
www.jerryhutchins.org